HEALING YOUR
FINANCIAL TRAUMA

People Cannot Build What They
Still Feel Unworthy of

Author/Editor: Rev. Darryl Bass

Electronic ISBN: 978-1-972115-14-5 (EPUB)
　　　　　　　　978-1-972115-33-6 (Kindle)
Paperback ISBN: 978-1-972115-15-2
Hardcover ISBN: 978-1-972115-16-9
Printed in the United States

The Library of Congress Control Number: 2026905725

Bass Publishing, LLC
Maywood, IL 60153

Disclaimer

The information contained in this book is for educational and informational purposes only. It is not intended as financial, legal, tax, medical, psychological, or professional advice. The author and publisher make no guarantees regarding the results that may be obtained from the use of this material.

All examples provided are illustrative and are not intended to represent or guarantee that any individual will achieve similar results. Personal growth, financial improvement, and life progression outcomes depend on individual effort, discipline, decisions, and circumstances.

Readers are encouraged to seek qualified professional advice regarding financial planning, legal matters, mental health, or other specialized areas before making decisions based on the information provided in this book.

The author and publisher disclaim any liability for any loss, risk, or damages, direct or indirect, that may arise from the use or application of the information contained herein.

Dedication

This book is dedicated to every person who has ever felt embarrassed by their financial story, overwhelmed by their financial mistakes, or uncertain about their financial future.

It is dedicated to the quiet warriors who worked tirelessly to provide for their families while carrying fears they never spoke aloud. It is dedicated to those who watched parents struggle and silently promised themselves that life would be different, even when they did not know how to make that difference possible.

This book is dedicated to those who believed stability was meant for someone else, who questioned their worth when financial challenges arose, and who carried shame connected to circumstances that were never truly their fault. Your story is not defined by the seasons where survival felt like your only option. Your story is defined by the courage it takes to heal, rebuild, and create a new financial legacy.

I dedicate this book to the children who will grow up in households shaped by healing rather than fear, by wisdom rather than confusion, and by stability rather than uncertainty. May they inherit peace because someone before them chose restoration over resignation.

And finally, this book is dedicated to you — the reader — who is willing to confront the past, embrace healing, and step boldly into the future you were always meant to build.

Acknowledgments

No journey of transformation happens in isolation, and this book exists because of the influence, encouragement, and wisdom of countless individuals who have contributed to my understanding of financial healing, emotional restoration, and personal growth.

I first acknowledge God, whose grace, wisdom, and divine guidance continually remind me that healing is always possible and restoration is always available. Every insight shared within these pages is rooted in the belief that transformation begins when individuals recognize their worth and align their lives with purpose and intentional stewardship.

I extend deep gratitude to the individuals, families, and communities who have allowed me to witness their financial struggles, victories, and healing journeys. Though their identities remain protected, their courage and transparency have shaped the lessons shared throughout this book. Your stories are living proof that financial trauma can be transformed into generational strength.

I am deeply thankful for the mentors, teachers, and leaders who challenged me to see money not only as a financial resource but as an emotional and spiritual responsibility. Your guidance has influenced my perspective and strengthened my commitment to helping others achieve stability, confidence, and legacy.

To my family, thank you for your patience, encouragement, and unwavering belief in my mission. Your support has provided the emotional and spiritual foundation that made this work possible. You remind me daily that financial healing is not simply about prosperity but about creating environments where love, security, and opportunity flourish across generations.

And to every reader who chooses to engage with this book, thank you for trusting this journey. Your willingness to confront difficult emotions and embrace transformation is the reason this message matters. You are not simply reading a book — you are participating in a movement toward generational restoration and empowered financial identity.

Foreword

Financial education has traditionally focused on numbers, strategies, and discipline. While those elements are essential, they often overlook a powerful truth: money is deeply connected to emotion, identity, and personal history. Many individuals struggle financially not because they lack knowledge or intelligence, but because unresolved emotional experiences influence their decisions in ways they rarely recognize.

Healing Your Financial Trauma addresses this overlooked reality by exploring the psychological and emotional foundations of financial behavior. It challenges readers to understand that financial struggles are often connected to experiences of instability, fear, or scarcity that shape subconscious beliefs about worth and security. By acknowledging these emotional influences, readers gain the opportunity to transform their relationship with money from survival-driven to purpose-driven.

Throughout this book, readers will encounter stories that reflect the complex and deeply personal nature of financial healing. These narratives illustrate how individuals from diverse backgrounds navigate trauma, rebuild confidence, and develop financial identities aligned with stability and legacy. The lessons shared extend beyond budgeting and wealth-building strategies, offering a holistic approach that integrates emotional healing, identity transformation, and visionary financial stewardship.

The journey presented in this book is both practical and inspirational. It encourages readers to confront internal barriers that prevent financial growth while providing motivation to pursue stability and generational impact. The message is clear: financial healing is not simply about accumulating wealth; it is about creating peace, confidence, and opportunity that extends beyond individual success.

Readers who engage with this book will discover that transformation begins with understanding their story and continues through intentional decisions that align with their purpose and values. The journey may require courage, reflection, and patience, but it ultimately leads to a level of financial and emotional freedom many individuals never realize is possible.

This book invites readers to see themselves not as victims of financial history but as architects of financial legacy. It offers hope, clarity, and empowerment for anyone willing to step beyond survival and embrace restoration.

Table of Contents

The Unseen Weight You've Been Carrying

Marcus never considered himself someone who struggled with money. On paper, he was doing better than most people he grew up with. He had a stable job managing logistics for a mid-sized distribution company, a decent apartment, and a car that still smelled new enough to make him feel like he was finally moving forward. Yet every time his phone buzzed with a banking notification, his chest tightened in a way he couldn't explain. He didn't avoid bills because he couldn't pay them. He avoided them because opening them triggered something deeper than math — it triggered memory.

Marcus grew up in a home where the last week of every month felt like walking through a thunderstorm with no shelter. His mother worked two jobs, but the stress of stretching income across rent, utilities, groceries, and unexpected emergencies filled their small apartment like invisible smoke. He remembers nights when his mother would sit silently at the kitchen table, calculator in one hand and unpaid envelopes scattered like fallen leaves across the table. She never cried in front of him, but he remembers the heaviness in her shoulders and the way her breathing would change when she thought he wasn't listening. Marcus learned early that money wasn't just currency — money was tension, anxiety, and emotional fragility. Now, as an adult, even when his bank balance was stable, his body reacted as if crisis was always approaching.

Financial trauma is often misunderstood because it doesn't leave visible bruises. It is stored quietly in emotional reflexes, subconscious expectations, and internal narratives about safety and survival. Many people believe financial struggle is purely about education or income, but trauma changes how the brain processes security. Trauma teaches the nervous system to anticipate danger even when danger is no longer present. Marcus would receive his paycheck and immediately pay every bill the same day, not because he lacked discipline, but because leaving money in his account made him anxious. Stability felt temporary. He wasn't managing finances; he was managing fear.

The unseen weight of financial trauma is carried by millions who have never named it. It shows up in people who work tirelessly but cannot rest, individuals who overspend during emotional distress, and families who avoid conversations about money because discussing it feels like reopening wounds. The struggle is rarely about numbers. It is about identity and worth. When people grow up surrounded by financial instability, they often internalize beliefs that they are destined to struggle or that wealth is reserved for others. These beliefs quietly guide decisions long before conscious planning begins. Financial trauma convinces people they must survive rather than build, endure rather than expand, and hustle rather than heal.

Consider Angela, a single mother who built a thriving catering business after years of working minimum-wage restaurant jobs. Her business eventually reached six figures, yet she constantly undercharged clients and avoided raising her prices despite increasing demand. Angela would often say she didn't want to appear greedy, but her hesitation stemmed from childhood experiences watching her father lose jobs repeatedly and her mother apologizing to creditors over the phone. Angela associated financial increase with instability. Charging more felt like tempting fate. When her mentor finally encouraged her to examine her pricing fears, Angela realized she wasn't afraid of losing clients — she was afraid of losing the fragile stability she had fought so hard to achieve.

The reality is that financial trauma rewires perception. People who have experienced prolonged financial insecurity often live in a constant state of hyper-vigilance. They scan for potential loss, expect disappointment, and struggle to celebrate success. Even blessings can trigger fear because trauma teaches people that good seasons are temporary. This emotional conditioning shapes spending habits, career decisions, and relationship dynamics. Individuals may stay in underpaying jobs because they fear risking stability. Others may chase rapid financial gain without long-term planning because survival thinking prioritizes immediate relief over strategic growth.

The most devastating effect of financial trauma is how it distorts self-worth. When individuals repeatedly experience lack, they may subconsciously believe they are unworthy of abundance. This belief influences how they negotiate salaries, pursue opportunities, and manage resources. Many people sabotage their financial progress not because they lack intelligence or discipline, but because their internal identity does not align with success. The mind cannot sustain what the heart feels undeserving of. Trauma whispers narratives that sound like truth: "People like you don't stay successful," or "If you have too much, something will take it away." These whispers become internal scripts that shape behavior in ways people rarely notice.

Healing begins with recognition. Understanding that financial trauma exists allows individuals to separate their identity from their experiences. Marcus eventually sought financial coaching after realizing his anxiety wasn't decreasing despite increasing income. Through guided reflection, he traced his reactions back to childhood memories of instability. For the first time, he recognized that his fear was a learned survival response rather than an accurate reflection of his present reality. That realization didn't instantly erase his anxiety, but it created space for transformation. He began building savings slowly, not just as a financial strategy but as a way of teaching his nervous system that safety could be consistent.

This book is an invitation to examine the unseen weight you may have been carrying for years. It is not about blaming your past or criticizing the survival strategies that helped you endure difficult seasons. Those strategies protected you when resources were limited and stability was fragile. However, survival is not meant to become a permanent identity. You were not created to live in constant financial fear or emotional exhaustion. You were created to build, expand, and experience peace. Healing financial trauma requires courage, honesty, and patience, but it also opens the door to a level of stability and freedom many people never realize is possible.

The journey you are beginning is not simply about improving financial habits. It is about reclaiming your sense of worth, redefining your relationship with money, and learning to build without fear shaping every decision. The weight you have been carrying is real, but it is not permanent. Naming the trauma is the first step toward releasing it.

Understanding your story allows you to rewrite it. And as you move forward, you will discover that healing financial trauma is not just about changing your bank account — it is about changing how you see yourself, your potential, and the life you deserve to build.

When Survival Becomes a Lifestyle

Tanya had never thought of herself as someone living in survival mode because survival was all she had ever known. She woke up before sunrise every morning, not because she enjoyed discipline but because waking up early felt like her only defense against life falling apart. Her routine was precise and rigid. Coffee brewed while she checked her email, her work schedule, and her bank balance in the same order every day. She worked as a dental assistant and carried herself with professionalism, warmth, and efficiency. Patients loved her. Her employer trusted her. Yet beneath her polished exterior lived a constant, low hum of anxiety that never fully turned off. Tanya grew up in a home where eviction notices arrived almost as regularly as the mail. Her mother was resilient but overwhelmed, juggling part-time jobs and unpredictable income streams that forced the family into frequent relocations. Each move meant starting over at new schools, losing friendships, and learning quickly that stability was temporary. As an adult, Tanya believed she had escaped that chaos, but her body still operated as if stability could collapse at any moment. She saved aggressively, avoided vacations, and worked overtime even when she didn't need the money, not realizing she had turned survival from a season into an identity.

Survival becomes dangerous when it stops being a response to crisis and starts shaping how a person sees life itself. Many individuals who grow up around financial uncertainty develop hyper-alert nervous systems that interpret peace as vulnerability rather than safety. Tanya struggled to relax during weekends because resting felt irresponsible. She declined social invitations and postponed personal goals because productivity felt like protection. Even when she reached financial milestones, such as paying off her student loans, she immediately replaced celebration with new worries. Survival thinking conditions people to measure security by how hard they are working rather than how stable their lives have become. This mindset often creates a paradox where individuals appear highly responsible but secretly feel exhausted and emotionally depleted. Financial trauma trains people to associate worth with constant effort, convincing them that slowing down invites disaster. Over time, this belief reshapes how they approach money, relationships, and personal identity. Instead of asking, "What life do I want to build?" survival-focused individuals ask, "What must I do to avoid falling apart?" The question itself reveals the depth of the trauma.

Another example of survival becoming identity can be seen in Derrick, a warehouse supervisor who prided himself on being the provider for his extended family. Derrick grew up watching his grandmother raise four children on a limited income while frequently borrowing money from relatives. He admired her strength and carried a deep internal vow never to let his family struggle the way she did. That vow motivated him to pursue stable employment, but it also locked him into fear-based decision-making. Derrick consistently turned down leadership promotions that required relocation because moving felt too risky, even though those opportunities would have doubled his salary. He justified his decisions by convincing himself that staying close to home was responsible, but beneath that logic lived an unspoken terror of financial collapse. Derrick spent years maintaining a stable but stagnant income while quietly resenting colleagues who advanced professionally. His survival identity protected him from risk, but it also limited his growth. He was working hard to maintain stability while unknowingly preventing expansion. His story illustrates how survival thinking often disguises itself as wisdom, making it difficult for individuals to recognize when fear is guiding their decisions.

Survival lifestyles also influence emotional spending patterns and money management habits. When people spend prolonged periods navigating instability, their brains learn to prioritize immediate relief over long-term planning. This pattern explains why some individuals who experience income increases still struggle to accumulate savings or invest strategically. Their subconscious belief system remains anchored in emergency thinking, prompting them to solve present discomfort rather than prepare for future security. Tanya experienced this pattern during a period when her employer offered performance bonuses. Instead of saving the extra income, she would spend it on home upgrades and gifts for family members, convincing herself she was improving her quality of life. In reality, she was attempting to create visible proof of stability to counter her internal fear of losing everything. Many people living in survival mode use spending as emotional reassurance rather than financial strategy. They purchase symbols of success to silence anxiety, not realizing those purchases often delay the long-term security they desire. Survival thinking narrows financial vision, keeping individuals focused on immediate emotional comfort instead of generational wealth building.

Breaking free from survival identity requires a profound shift in internal permission. Individuals must learn that they are allowed to move beyond crisis living without betraying their past or disrespecting the resilience that carried them through hardship. Tanya's turning point came when she attended a workplace financial wellness seminar, expecting to receive budgeting tips but instead hearing a therapist discuss the psychological impact of scarcity environments. During the session, the therapist explained how trauma can trap people in productivity addiction, making them equate rest with irresponsibility. Tanya felt exposed and relieved simultaneously. For the first time, she considered the possibility that her relentless work ethic was not purely discipline but also unresolved fear. She began experimenting with small behavioral changes, such as leaving work on time and allocating a small portion of her income toward experiences she previously considered indulgent. Those changes initially triggered anxiety, but over time, they helped her nervous system recognize that stability could coexist with enjoyment. Tanya discovered that building wealth requires emotional regulation as much as financial knowledge. Her healing did not erase her discipline; it transformed it into intentional, balanced stewardship.

Survival is often celebrated in motivational narratives, but survival alone is not the destination. Survival is the foundation upon which stability, peace, and expansion are meant to be built. Many individuals remain trapped in survival identity because society praises hustle culture without acknowledging its emotional cost. While perseverance is admirable, constant urgency can prevent individuals from experiencing the very security they are working to achieve. Derrick eventually faced his survival identity when his younger cousin asked him why he never pursued management roles despite his experience. The question forced him to confront fears he had disguised as practicality. Through counseling and mentorship, Derrick began reframing risk as opportunity rather than threat. He accepted a regional supervisory role that required relocation, a decision that initially terrified him but ultimately increased his income, professional confidence, and financial flexibility. Derrick learned that growth often requires stepping beyond familiar survival environments and trusting that stability can be maintained through wisdom rather than constant control.

Recognizing when survival has become a lifestyle is one of the most powerful steps toward financial healing. It invites individuals to examine their relationship with effort, rest, risk, and worth. Survival once protected you, but protection is not meant to become a permanent identity. You were not created to live in constant alertness, waiting for the next crisis to prove your strength. You were created to build a life where peace is not temporary and stability does not feel fragile. As you continue this journey, you will begin learning how to transition from survival-driven decisions to purpose-driven planning. The next chapter will explore how shame quietly shapes financial identity and influences the internal narratives that determine how individuals see their worth and potential, revealing why many people struggle to believe they deserve the very stability they are working so hard to achieve.

How Shame Shapes Your Money Identity

Shame rarely announces itself loudly. It does not enter a room demanding attention or screaming accusations. Instead, it arrives quietly, often disguised as self-awareness or humility, weaving itself into the internal dialogue people repeat without questioning. For Julian, shame became a silent companion long before he understood its influence over his financial life. Julian was the first in his family to graduate college, earning a degree in marketing that promised opportunity and upward mobility. He secured a corporate position within a year, purchased a modest home, and began building the life he had once imagined while watching his parents struggle to pay bills during his childhood. From the outside, Julian represented progress. Inside, he felt like an impostor waiting to be exposed. He obsessively compared himself to coworkers from wealthier backgrounds, believing they possessed knowledge he lacked and confidence he did not deserve. Every financial decision, from negotiating salary to investing, triggered an internal voice reminding him he was "lucky to be there." Julian's achievements did not silence that voice because shame does not measure success by reality; it measures worth by past wounds.

Shame around money often originates from early experiences where financial hardship was linked to personal failure or emotional embarrassment. Many individuals grow up in households where money struggles are accompanied by blame, secrecy, or tension, creating powerful emotional associations that persist into adulthood. Julian remembered overhearing arguments between his parents about overdue utilities, each conversation ending with apologies and quiet resignation. His father would often say, "I should have done better," while his mother reassured him that they would figure things out, though her trembling voice revealed uncertainty. Those moments taught Julian that financial struggle was not simply a circumstance but a reflection of personal inadequacy. As an adult, he internalized the belief that financial success required perfection and that any mistake would confirm his fear of being inherently flawed. Shame transforms financial challenges into identity crises, convincing individuals that errors in budgeting, investing, or earning are proof of personal failure rather than opportunities for growth. This emotional distortion prevents many people from taking necessary financial risks or seeking guidance because admitting confusion feels like confirming their deepest insecurity.

The power of shame lies in its ability to rewrite personal narratives. Individuals affected by financial shame often develop self-limiting beliefs that influence how they negotiate opportunities and manage wealth. Julian consistently accepted smaller raises than his performance warranted because advocating for higher compensation felt arrogant and undeserved. He volunteered for additional responsibilities without requesting title promotions, convincing himself that proving his dedication was more important than requesting recognition. His managers appreciated his work ethic, but his reluctance to assert his value slowed his career growth. Financial shame frequently leads individuals to underprice their skills, tolerate exploitative work environments, or avoid entrepreneurial ventures due to fear of visible failure. These behaviors are rarely conscious decisions. They are protective mechanisms developed to avoid the emotional pain associated with feeling unworthy. Shame convinces individuals that invisibility is safer than visibility, that modesty is safer than ambition, and that maintaining stability is safer than pursuing expansion. Over time, these beliefs create invisible ceilings that limit earning potential and wealth accumulation.

Danielle's story illustrates how financial shame can influence spending behaviors as well as earning decisions. Danielle worked as a nurse, a career she chose because it offered stability and emotional fulfillment. She excelled professionally and maintained a steady income, yet she struggled with compulsive luxury purchases whenever she experienced emotional distress. Growing up, Danielle's family frequently moved between relatives' homes after her mother lost employment during economic downturns. She often wore donated clothing and avoided social events because she felt embarrassed by her appearance. As an adult, designer clothing and expensive accessories became symbols of security and self-worth. Danielle rationalized her purchases as rewards for her demanding job, but she later realized those spending habits were attempts to erase childhood humiliation. Financial shame often fuels emotional spending because individuals unconsciously attempt to replace internal inadequacy with external validation. The temporary confidence gained from material upgrades rarely resolves the underlying wound, leading to cycles of spending followed by guilt and self-criticism. Danielle's turning point came when she recognized that her purchases were conversations with her past rather than celebrations of her present. Understanding that distinction allowed her to confront the emotional roots of her financial habits rather than continuing to treat symptoms through consumption.

Shame also shapes how individuals receive financial blessings or assistance. Many people with financial trauma struggle to accept help because receiving support triggers feelings of weakness or dependency. Julian experienced this conflict when his company offered mentorship programs designed to accelerate leadership development. Although he qualified, he declined participation, fearing that requesting guidance would reveal incompetence. His decision reflected a common consequence of financial shame: individuals avoid resources that could accelerate growth because they associate asking for help with confirming inadequacy. Healing financial shame requires redefining vulnerability as strength rather than weakness. When Julian eventually accepted mentorship after a supervisor encouraged him to reconsider, he discovered that his peers faced similar insecurities regardless of background. That realization challenged his belief that he was uniquely unprepared for success. Danielle experienced a similar transformation after attending financial therapy sessions recommended by a colleague. Through guided conversations, she explored the emotional triggers connected to her spending patterns and learned that acknowledging her struggles did not diminish her competence or independence. Instead, it strengthened her ability to make intentional financial decisions grounded in self-respect rather than emotional compensation.

Breaking financial shame involves rewriting internal identity scripts that were formed during vulnerable life stages. Individuals must learn to separate their worth from their financial history and recognize that early experiences shaped their coping strategies but do not define their future capacity. This process often requires patience and compassionate self-examination because shame thrives in secrecy and self-judgment. Julian began practicing salary negotiations through role-playing exercises with his mentor, gradually building confidence to advocate for his value. Danielle created spending plans that included discretionary purchases without emotional urgency, allowing her to enjoy financial rewards without guilt or impulsivity. Both discovered that healing financial shame does not eliminate discipline or ambition; it transforms them into expressions of self-worth rather than attempts to prove worthiness. When individuals release shame, they begin making decisions aligned with long-term stability rather than short-term emotional relief. They pursue opportunities with curiosity rather than fear, recognizing that mistakes are part of growth rather than evidence of inadequacy.

Understanding how shame shapes money identity reveals why financial transformation requires emotional healing alongside practical strategy. Shame distorts perception, convincing individuals they must earn the right to security through perfection or relentless effort. True financial healing begins when individuals accept that their worth exists independently of their financial past. As this journey continues, the next chapter will explore how generational patterns silently influence financial behavior, examining how beliefs and emotional responses are inherited through observation and environment, and how breaking those cycles creates the possibility for lasting stability and legacy transformation.

The Generational Echo

The silence in Harold's childhood home was louder than any argument he had ever heard. His family rarely spoke openly about money, yet the presence of financial strain hovered in every corner of the house like a storm waiting to break. Harold remembered the way his mother stretched meals to last several days, quietly substituting ingredients while insisting everything tasted the same. He remembered the careful way his father folded overdue bills and placed them in a kitchen drawer as if hiding them might reduce their urgency. No one explained their situation, but Harold learned early that money was something fragile, unpredictable, and emotionally heavy. As he grew older, he carried those silent lessons with him into adulthood without realizing they had shaped his beliefs about security and success. When Harold eventually built a career in construction management, earning more than either of his parents ever had, he found himself unable to enjoy his financial progress. Every promotion felt temporary, every savings milestone felt vulnerable, and every unexpected expense triggered anxiety far greater than the situation required. Harold believed he was protecting himself by staying cautious, never recognizing that he was reacting to inherited fear rather than present reality.

Financial trauma often travels through families in subtle ways that are rarely acknowledged or discussed. Generational financial patterns are passed down through observation, emotional tone, and behavioral modeling long before children understand concepts like budgeting or investment. Harold did not inherit debt from his parents, but he inherited their fear of financial instability and their tendency to equate survival with success. Children raised in environments where money is associated with stress often internalize those emotions as foundational truths about adulthood. They learn to view financial security as temporary and financial growth as risky. These inherited beliefs influence career choices, spending habits, and even relationship dynamics. Harold consistently chose stable but limiting job opportunities because security felt safer than advancement. He declined entrepreneurial ventures despite possessing strong leadership skills, convincing himself that avoiding risk was responsible decision-making. In reality, his choices reflected a subconscious loyalty to the survival mindset modeled during his childhood. Generational financial trauma often operates as an invisible script, guiding decisions through fear disguised as practicality.

Leah experienced generational financial trauma in a different but equally powerful way. Raised by a grandmother who survived economic hardship during multiple recessions, Leah grew up hearing constant warnings about the unpredictability of financial success. Her grandmother emphasized saving above all else, often repeating stories about families who lost everything after brief periods of prosperity. Leah admired her grandmother's resilience and adopted her caution as wisdom. As an adult, Leah built a successful career as a graphic designer, eventually launching her own freelance business. Despite her consistent income growth, she lived in a small apartment she had outgrown years earlier and avoided hiring assistants who could expand her workload capacity. Leah convinced herself that minimizing expenses was the key to long-term stability. Her hesitation to reinvest in her business stemmed not from financial ignorance but from generational caution passed down through stories of loss. Leah's grandmother had survived instability by preserving resources, and Leah unconsciously honored that survival strategy even though her circumstances allowed for growth. Generational financial trauma often creates loyalty conflicts where individuals feel guilty for pursuing opportunities that exceed the limitations experienced by previous generations.

Breaking generational financial cycles requires recognizing that inherited beliefs were formed in response to specific historical and environmental challenges. Harold's parents navigated unstable employment markets and limited access to financial education, developing survival strategies necessary for their circumstances. Leah's grandmother endured economic collapses that reinforced the importance of preservation over expansion. These survival approaches were acts of strength, not failure. However, survival strategies designed for one generation may restrict the growth potential of the next if they are followed without evaluation. Individuals raised within financially cautious environments often struggle with expansion because growth can feel like betrayal rather than progress. Harold wrestled with guilt when considering relocation for higher-paying leadership roles because leaving his hometown felt like abandoning his family's legacy of endurance. Leah hesitated to increase her service rates because she feared appearing disconnected from her family's history of financial humility. These emotional conflicts illustrate how generational trauma influences identity and decision-making, often creating internal resistance to opportunities that align with present capacity.

Transformation began for Harold when he attended a professional leadership conference that included sessions on generational wealth building. During a panel discussion, a speaker described how honoring family resilience involves expanding opportunities rather than repeating limitations. That statement challenged Harold's understanding of loyalty and responsibility. He began reflecting on how his parents' sacrifices were intended to create options he never allowed himself to pursue. Through financial counseling and career coaching, Harold gradually reframed risk as stewardship rather than danger. He accepted a regional project director position that required relocating, a decision that initially triggered anxiety but ultimately increased his income, leadership confidence, and ability to support his extended family in ways previously impossible. Leah experienced her transformation after a mentor encouraged her to examine how her grandmother's survival lessons influenced her business decisions. By acknowledging that her grandmother's caution protected her during economic uncertainty but did not need to define Leah's future, she began investing in marketing and hiring part-time design assistants. Her business expanded rapidly, allowing her to build savings while experiencing professional fulfillment she had previously denied herself.

Generational financial trauma often persists because it remains unnamed. Families rarely discuss emotional relationships with money, focusing instead on practical survival techniques without addressing the psychological impact of scarcity or instability. Breaking these cycles requires individuals to examine inherited beliefs with compassion rather than criticism. Harold learned to appreciate his parents' resilience while recognizing that their fear-based caution no longer needed to guide his decisions. Leah honored her grandmother's wisdom while allowing herself to build a business that reflected her present opportunities rather than past limitations. Both discovered that healing generational trauma involves preserving family strength while releasing inherited fear. This process transforms survival narratives into empowerment narratives, allowing individuals to build financial stability that honors past sacrifices while expanding future possibilities. Understanding generational financial trauma reveals that financial behavior is rarely shaped by individual experiences alone. It is influenced by family history, cultural narratives, and environmental survival strategies passed down through observation and storytelling. Recognizing these influences allows individuals to consciously decide which beliefs to preserve and which to release. As this journey continues, the next chapter will explore emotional spending and the subconscious search for safety, revealing how unresolved financial trauma often manifests through purchasing behaviors that attempt to soothe emotional wounds rather than create long-term security.

Emotional Spending and the Search for Safety

Elena always described herself as responsible with money, a description supported by her steady career as a project coordinator for a healthcare company and her reputation among friends as someone who rarely missed payments or financial obligations. Yet late at night, when stress from deadlines and workplace expectations lingered long after her laptop closed, Elena often found herself scrolling through online stores, adding items to her cart with a sense of urgency she struggled to explain. The purchases were rarely extravagant or reckless enough to raise alarm, but they occurred with a consistency that left her confused and occasionally ashamed. Growing up, Elena had lived through years of emotional instability caused by her parents' unpredictable employment and frequent arguments about finances. Her childhood home felt emotionally fragile, and she learned early to find comfort in small material rewards such as new school supplies or occasional shopping trips that temporarily replaced tension with excitement. As an adult,

Elena believed she had outgrown those coping habits, but her purchasing behavior revealed a deeper truth. Each online order provided a brief sense of control and reassurance, a momentary belief that life was stable and manageable. She was not buying products as much as she was buying relief from emotional discomfort.

Emotional spending develops when individuals learn to associate financial transactions with emotional regulation. When financial trauma is present, spending can become a subconscious strategy for creating temporary safety or validation. Elena's late-night shopping rituals were not impulsive decisions rooted in carelessness but rather protective behaviors developed during vulnerable developmental years. The human brain seeks patterns that reduce discomfort, and for many individuals who experience instability, spending becomes a learned method of creating positive emotional shifts. Elena noticed that purchases felt most satisfying during periods of high stress or loneliness, reinforcing a neurological connection between consumption and emotional relief. Over time, this pattern reshaped her financial habits, diverting income away from long-term savings goals while maintaining the illusion of self-care. Emotional spending often disguises itself as deserved reward or lifestyle improvement, making it difficult for individuals to recognize its connection to unresolved trauma. The relief it provides is genuine but temporary, leaving underlying insecurities unaddressed and often intensifying guilt once financial consequences appear.

Michael experienced emotional spending through a different emotional pathway. As a child, he watched his parents navigate prolonged unemployment during an economic downturn, leading to years of financial scarcity that limited basic family experiences. Michael remembered declining invitations to social events and extracurricular activities because his family could not afford participation fees. He internalized those limitations as evidence that financial success was necessary for personal worth and social acceptance. As an adult working in sales, Michael achieved substantial income growth, but he struggled to control his spending on luxury experiences, including high-end electronics, expensive dining, and frequent travel. These purchases created the identity he believed financial success required, allowing him to rewrite his childhood narrative of exclusion. Michael justified his spending as motivation for continued professional success, yet he often experienced anxiety when reviewing his bank statements, recognizing that his consumption habits were preventing meaningful wealth accumulation. Emotional spending frequently emerges as an attempt to repair past deprivation, replacing earlier feelings of embarrassment or exclusion with visible markers of success. Michael was not spending irresponsibly in his mind; he was attempting to erase childhood shame through adult financial expression.

Emotional spending often persists because it addresses emotional pain that individuals may not consciously recognize. Financial trauma teaches individuals to associate money with security, status, or self-worth, creating powerful emotional motivations behind purchasing decisions. Elena began noticing that her spending increased after emotionally draining work meetings or during periods of social isolation. The packages arriving at her apartment provided anticipation and excitement, temporarily replacing exhaustion with satisfaction. Michael experienced similar emotional cycles, particularly after achieving professional milestones. Instead of celebrating with intentional financial planning, he engaged in celebratory spending that reinforced his identity as someone who had escaped financial hardship. Emotional spending patterns are rarely about material desire alone; they represent attempts to regulate internal emotional states shaped by past instability. These behaviors often persist because they provide immediate gratification, making it difficult for individuals to recognize their long-term financial consequences. Without emotional awareness, spending decisions can become automatic responses to stress, loneliness, or insecurity rather than intentional financial choices aligned with future goals.

Transformation for Elena began when she attended a corporate wellness seminar focused on financial psychology rather than budgeting techniques. During the session, the speaker explained how financial habits often mirror emotional coping mechanisms developed during childhood. Elena recognized her late-night shopping routine in the examples presented and felt a mixture of embarrassment and relief. She began tracking her emotional state before making purchases, discovering consistent patterns linking spending to fatigue and stress rather than actual financial need. Through therapy and financial coaching, Elena developed alternative coping strategies such as journaling and structured relaxation routines that replaced the emotional function spending had served. These changes initially felt uncomfortable because they removed her immediate source of emotional relief, but over time they allowed her to redirect financial resources toward savings and personal development. Michael experienced his breakthrough after attending a financial planning session where his advisor asked him to describe what success meant beyond visible lifestyle upgrades. The question forced him to confront how much of his spending was motivated by childhood experiences of exclusion. By acknowledging that his purchases were attempts to rewrite past emotional wounds, Michael began creating intentional financial plans that balanced enjoyment with long-term wealth building. He discovered that emotional fulfillment could be achieved through experiences and relationships rather than material validation alone.

Emotional spending is not evidence of financial irresponsibility but often a reflection of unresolved emotional needs. Individuals who grew up navigating financial trauma frequently develop subconscious beliefs that money can compensate for emotional instability or personal inadequacy. Recognizing these patterns requires compassion and curiosity rather than judgment. Elena learned that her spending habits were attempts to comfort a younger version of herself that once felt overwhelmed and powerless. Michael realized that his luxury purchases were efforts to secure social belonging and personal validation. Both discovered that healing financial trauma involves addressing emotional wounds directly rather than masking them through consumption. By replacing reactive spending with intentional financial planning and emotional self-awareness, they transformed their relationship with money from survival-driven to purpose-driven. Emotional spending loses its power when individuals learn to create internal safety rather than purchasing external reassurance.

Understanding emotional spending reveals the intricate relationship between trauma, identity, and financial behavior. Money often becomes a language through which individuals attempt to communicate unmet emotional needs or rewrite painful memories. Healing requires learning to recognize those emotional messages and responding with awareness rather than automatic consumption. As this journey continues, the next chapter will explore attachment and avoidance money personalities, examining how individuals develop contrasting financial behaviors rooted in the same foundational trauma and how balancing those responses creates sustainable financial stability and emotional peace.

Attachment and Avoidance: The Two Money Personalities

Daniel prided himself on being cautious with money, a quality he described as responsibility and discipline. He maintained meticulous spreadsheets tracking every expense, checked his bank account multiple times a day, and rarely made purchases without extensive research. Friends often admired his financial control, occasionally seeking advice on budgeting or saving strategies. Yet beneath Daniel's structured approach lived an anxiety he struggled to explain. Growing up, Daniel witnessed his parents lose their family business during a sudden market collapse, forcing them to sell their home and move into a small rental apartment. He remembered the night his father packed boxes in silence while his mother reassured him that everything would be fine, though her trembling hands betrayed uncertainty. Those memories imprinted a powerful belief that financial security could disappear without warning. As an adult, Daniel equated control with safety, believing that constant monitoring of his finances protected him from repeating his parents' loss. He accumulated savings far beyond his immediate needs but resisted investing or making lifestyle improvements, convinced that releasing money created vulnerability. Daniel did not realize that his financial attachment was rooted in fear rather than confidence, transforming his relationship with money into one of protection rather than stewardship.

Financial attachment develops when individuals respond to financial trauma by seeking security through control and accumulation. People who adopt this money personality often associate stability with maintaining absolute authority over financial outcomes. Daniel's cautious behavior allowed him to build impressive savings, but it also limited his quality of life and long-term wealth potential. He declined investment opportunities recommended by financial advisors because market fluctuations triggered memories of his family's business failure. He postponed personal goals such as purchasing a home or traveling internationally because spending money felt like inviting instability. Financial attachment often appears responsible from an external perspective, but internally it can create chronic anxiety and emotional rigidity. Individuals with attachment personalities may struggle to trust financial systems, partnerships, or even their own decision-making, believing that personal control is the only reliable defense against loss. This belief can prevent them from participating in wealth-building opportunities that require calculated risk and long-term vision. Attachment personalities often excel at preserving resources but may struggle to expand them because growth requires trust and strategic vulnerability.

In contrast, Lauren developed an avoidance money personality shaped by her own experiences with financial instability. Lauren grew up in a household where money conversations frequently escalated into emotional conflict between her parents. She associated financial discussions with arguments, blame, and emotional exhaustion, leading her to disconnect from money management as a form of self-protection. As an adult working as a freelance photographer, Lauren earned a fluctuating but generally sufficient income, yet she avoided tracking expenses or planning long-term savings. Bills were often paid at the last possible moment, and financial planning felt overwhelming and emotionally draining. Lauren convinced herself that focusing on her creative career required flexibility and spontaneity, masking her deeper discomfort with financial structure. Avoidance personalities often respond to financial trauma by distancing themselves from money-related responsibilities, believing that disengagement reduces emotional stress. Lauren's avoidance allowed her to escape immediate anxiety but created long-term instability that reinforced her fear of financial conversations. She experienced recurring cycles of financial pressure followed by temporary relief, never recognizing that her avoidance behaviors perpetuated the instability she feared.

Attachment and avoidance personalities represent opposing responses to the same underlying trauma: fear of instability and emotional vulnerability connected to financial uncertainty. Daniel attempted to eliminate fear through excessive control, while Lauren attempted to eliminate fear through emotional distance. Both strategies developed as protective mechanisms during vulnerable life stages and initially provided psychological comfort. Over time, however, these coping patterns created limitations that prevented sustainable financial growth. Daniel's attachment limited his willingness to pursue investment opportunities that could create generational wealth. Lauren's avoidance prevented her from establishing consistent financial systems necessary for stability. Financial trauma often produces polarized behaviors because the brain seeks certainty, either by maintaining rigid control or by disengaging from perceived threats entirely. Neither extreme provides balanced financial health because sustainable wealth requires both discipline and flexibility. Recognizing these personality patterns allows individuals to understand that their financial behaviors are not character flaws but learned survival responses that can be transformed through awareness and intentional practice.

Daniel's transformation began during a leadership retreat organized by his employer, where a guest speaker discussed the emotional psychology of money. During a group exercise, participants were asked to describe their earliest memory of financial fear. Daniel shared the story of his family's business collapse, experiencing emotional vulnerability he had suppressed for years. The facilitator introduced the concept that financial control can become a protective cage rather than a shield, preventing individuals from experiencing both growth and enjoyment. Daniel realized that his savings had become symbolic armor protecting him from emotional pain rather than tools for purposeful expansion. He began working with a financial planner who introduced gradual investment strategies designed to build confidence rather than trigger anxiety. Daniel started with small, diversified investments that allowed him to experience market fluctuations without overwhelming fear. Over time, he developed trust in financial systems and his own decision-making abilities, discovering that stewardship involved both preservation and expansion. His transformation did not eliminate his disciplined nature but redirected it toward balanced financial growth and intentional lifestyle improvements.

Lauren's transformation emerged through an unexpected conversation with a longtime client who noticed her financial stress during a photography project. The client, who owned a small business, shared her own history of financial avoidance and how she overcame it through structured planning and mentorship. Lauren reluctantly agreed to meet with a financial coach, expecting criticism but encountering empathy and psychological insight instead. The coach helped Lauren create simplified financial systems tailored to her freelance income structure, including automated bill payments and flexible savings plans aligned with her fluctuating earnings. Initially, Lauren felt discomfort confronting financial details she had avoided for years, but consistent guidance helped her develop confidence and emotional resilience. She discovered that financial structure reduced stress rather than increasing it, allowing her to focus more fully on her creative work without recurring financial crises. Lauren's avoidance personality gradually shifted toward balanced engagement, demonstrating that emotional healing can transform financial behaviors without sacrificing individuality or lifestyle flexibility.

Attachment and avoidance personalities reveal how deeply financial trauma influences emotional responses to money management. Both Daniel and Lauren learned that healing requires moving toward balance rather than eliminating protective instincts entirely. Daniel retained his attention to detail while learning to embrace strategic risk, and Lauren preserved her creative independence while developing structured financial habits. Their journeys illustrate that financial health emerges when individuals integrate discipline with trust, allowing money to function as a tool for purposeful living rather than emotional protection or avoidance. Occasionally, moments of reflection led both Daniel and Lauren to recognize how releasing fear allowed them to experience a deeper sense of peace and clarity, suggesting that emotional healing often opens pathways to stability that practical strategies alone cannot achieve. As this journey continues, the next chapter will explore the internal conflict between the need to prove self-worth through financial success and the fear of becoming the person capable of sustaining that success, revealing how identity transformation influences long-term financial stability.

The Need to Prove vs. The Fear of Becoming

Calvin had spent most of his adult life chasing achievement with relentless determination, believing success was the only way to rewrite the story of his upbringing. Raised in a household where financial instability was constant, Calvin grew up watching his parents juggle part-time jobs while reminding him that education was his only escape from struggle. Their encouragement was sincere, but it carried an unspoken urgency that shaped Calvin's sense of identity. He excelled academically, earned scholarships, and eventually secured a high-paying position in corporate finance. From the outside, Calvin represented everything his family had hoped he would become. Yet internally, he carried a restless pressure that never allowed him to feel satisfied with his accomplishments. Each promotion provided temporary relief before being replaced by new goals, longer work hours, and deeper anxiety about maintaining his status. Calvin convinced himself that his drive was ambition, but he secretly feared that slowing down would expose him as someone who did not belong in the world he had entered. His success was not simply professional advancement; it was an ongoing attempt to prove he was worthy of stability, recognition, and respect. The need to prove financial worth often develops when individuals grow up equating survival with validation. Calvin's childhood taught him that security was conditional and easily lost, creating a subconscious belief that his value depended on constant performance. This mindset drove him to exceed expectations professionally but prevented him from experiencing fulfillment. He measured his worth through external achievements rather than internal stability, leading to chronic exhaustion and emotional isolation. The need to prove oneself can create a cycle where individuals continuously pursue success without allowing themselves to enjoy it. Calvin avoided vacations, delayed personal relationships, and neglected hobbies because rest felt irresponsible and distractions felt dangerous. Financial trauma frequently produces individuals who are outwardly successful but inwardly anxious, constantly seeking reassurance through productivity. The need to prove is fueled by fear disguised as motivation, convincing individuals that their value exists only as long as their performance remains flawless. This belief creates fragile success, where achievements provide recognition but rarely provide peace.

While Calvin struggled with the need to prove himself, Naomi experienced the opposite but equally limiting response to financial trauma: the fear of becoming someone capable of sustaining success. Naomi grew up in a modest household where financial security fluctuated depending on seasonal employment patterns affecting her family's income. She developed a strong work ethic and eventually built a thriving small business designing event décor. Her creativity attracted high-profile clients, and her revenue increased steadily, yet Naomi repeatedly declined opportunities to expand her company. She resisted hiring staff, avoided marketing campaigns, and rejected partnership offers that could significantly increase her visibility and earnings. Naomi convinced herself she preferred simplicity and independence, but deeper reflection revealed a fear that expansion would expose her to failure or public scrutiny. Success introduced unfamiliar expectations and responsibilities that challenged her comfort with predictable routines. Naomi feared that becoming a business leader with employees and public recognition would transform her identity into someone she did not recognize or trust. Financial trauma can create internal resistance to growth because transformation requires individuals to release familiar survival identities and embrace unfamiliar leadership roles. The conflict between proving and becoming reflects a deeper identity struggle rooted in financial trauma. Calvin believed he had to constantly demonstrate competence to secure his place in professional environments, while Naomi feared that expanding her success would demand personal transformation she felt unprepared to handle. Both responses originate from subconscious beliefs formed during vulnerable life stages. Calvin associated achievement with safety, believing that failure would return him to instability. Naomi associated visibility with vulnerability, fearing that success would expose her to judgment or loss. These identity conflicts often operate beneath conscious awareness, influencing financial decisions through emotional reflexes rather than intentional strategy. Individuals caught between proving and fearing transformation may oscillate between overworking and self-sabotaging, creating inconsistent financial progress despite strong talent or opportunity. Calvin occasionally declined leadership roles that required delegating responsibility, believing he needed to maintain personal control to ensure success. Naomi accepted prestigious projects but limited their scale, preventing her business from reaching its full potential. Their behaviors reflected internal dialogues shaped by financial trauma, demonstrating how identity beliefs influence professional and financial outcomes.

Calvin's transformation began unexpectedly during a company leadership seminar focused on sustainable career growth. A speaker challenged participants to identify whether their motivation stemmed from purpose or fear, prompting Calvin to reflect on his relentless work habits. He realized that his achievements had been attempts to outrun insecurity rather than expressions of passion or vision. Through executive coaching, Calvin began redefining success as stability and balance rather than constant advancement. He learned to delegate responsibilities, take scheduled vacations, and invest in long-term financial planning that supported personal well-being. The process felt uncomfortable because it required releasing his identity as someone who proved worth through performance. Over time, Calvin discovered that allowing himself to rest strengthened his professional effectiveness and emotional health. Naomi's transformation emerged through mentorship from a seasoned entrepreneur who recognized her hesitation to expand. The mentor encouraged Naomi to view leadership as stewardship rather than transformation of identity. Naomi gradually introduced small business expansions, hiring part-time assistants and implementing marketing strategies that increased client visibility without overwhelming her. She learned that becoming a leader did not erase her creative independence but expanded her influence and financial stability.

The need to prove and the fear of becoming illustrate how financial trauma influences identity formation and professional decision-making. Calvin and Naomi both learned that healing required redefining their relationship with success and self-worth. Calvin discovered that his value existed independently of constant achievement, allowing him to pursue goals aligned with personal fulfillment rather than insecurity. Naomi realized that growth required embracing transformation as an extension of her identity rather than a threat to it. Their journeys demonstrate that financial healing involves balancing ambition with emotional confidence, allowing individuals to pursue success without attaching their worth to performance or fearing the responsibilities that accompany growth. Occasionally, moments of reflection helped both Calvin and Naomi recognize that releasing fear allowed them to experience a sense of clarity and peace that extended beyond financial achievement, suggesting that true stability often emerges when identity evolves alongside opportunity.

Understanding the conflict between proving and becoming reveals the complex relationship between financial trauma and personal identity. Individuals shaped by scarcity often carry internal narratives that equate success with pressure or vulnerability, preventing them from fully embracing growth opportunities. Healing requires learning that financial stability does not require constant validation or identity sacrifice. As this journey continues, the next chapter will explore how scarcity can become emotionally familiar, examining why individuals sometimes remain attached to financial struggle even when stability becomes attainable and how releasing that attachment allows them to step fully into sustainable prosperity.

When Scarcity Feels Like Home

Trevor never described his life as unstable, even though stability was something he had rarely experienced growing up. He considered himself adaptable, proud of his ability to adjust quickly to unexpected challenges and financial setbacks. Trevor worked as an automotive technician, a career he built through determination rather than formal education. His income fluctuated depending on overtime opportunities and seasonal demand, but he consistently managed to pay his bills and support his lifestyle. Despite his hard work, Trevor noticed a pattern he could not explain. Whenever his savings account reached a comfortable level, unexpected expenses or impulsive decisions seemed to reduce his balance almost immediately. Sometimes it was a sudden car upgrade he convinced himself was necessary for reliability. Other times it was an unplanned vacation he justified as well-deserved rest after months of overtime. Trevor rarely felt regret in the moment, but he experienced frustration afterward when he realized his progress toward financial security had once again disappeared. Growing up in a household where financial strain was constant,

Trevor learned to expect instability as part of life. His parents navigated recurring layoffs and mounting bills, often reassuring him that they would figure things out despite visible stress. As an adult, Trevor unconsciously recreated that cycle, maintaining a financial lifestyle that felt familiar even when it prevented him from building lasting stability.

Scarcity can become emotionally comfortable because it reflects the environment in which many individuals learn to survive. When financial instability shapes childhood experiences, the brain adapts by recognizing struggle as predictable and manageable. Stability, on the other hand, can feel unfamiliar and uncertain because it lacks the emotional patterns the brain associates with control. Trevor felt confident navigating financial emergencies because crisis situations mirrored his upbringing, where problem-solving under pressure was normal. When his finances improved, he experienced subtle discomfort that often led him to make decisions that reintroduced financial urgency. This subconscious behavior is common among individuals who have experienced financial trauma. The brain seeks emotional familiarity, even if that familiarity involves stress or limitation. Scarcity becomes a psychological comfort zone where individuals feel prepared and capable, while stability introduces uncertainty that challenges long-standing survival identities. Trevor's spending decisions were not reckless attempts to sabotage progress but unconscious efforts to return to emotional environments he understood how to navigate.

Marissa experienced scarcity comfort through a different emotional pathway. Raised in a family where financial survival required constant sacrifice, Marissa developed a deep appreciation for frugality and resourcefulness. Her parents worked tirelessly to provide basic necessities, often postponing personal goals and celebrations to maintain household stability. Marissa admired their resilience and carried those values into adulthood, building a successful career as a paralegal. Despite her consistent income and disciplined saving habits, Marissa struggled to allow herself to enjoy financial milestones. She avoided purchasing quality furniture for her home, postponed travel opportunities, and resisted lifestyle improvements that reflected her professional achievements.

Marissa believed maintaining minimal expenses honored her parents' sacrifices, but her reluctance to experience financial comfort created emotional tension she could not explain. She felt guilt when considering purchases that symbolized stability, as if enjoying financial security meant forgetting the struggle that shaped her family's identity. Scarcity often becomes intertwined with loyalty, convincing individuals that embracing abundance dishonors past hardship. Marissa's financial restraint preserved savings but limited her ability to experience the emotional peace she worked diligently to achieve.

The emotional familiarity of scarcity is reinforced by societal narratives that romanticize struggle as evidence of strength and resilience. Trevor frequently received praise from friends and coworkers for his ability to handle financial emergencies without visible stress, reinforcing his identity as someone who thrived under pressure. Marissa received admiration for her disciplined saving habits and modest lifestyle, further validating her reluctance to enjoy financial stability. While resilience and discipline are valuable qualities, they can become barriers when individuals feel obligated to maintain struggle to preserve their sense of identity or social approval. Financial trauma often creates subconscious beliefs that comfort and abundance are temporary or undeserved, leading individuals to recreate scarcity through spending habits, career decisions, or lifestyle limitations. Trevor occasionally declined training opportunities that could increase his earning potential because additional responsibility felt unfamiliar and risky. Marissa avoided promotions that required relocation, fearing that lifestyle changes associated with higher income would disconnect her from her family's history. Both individuals unconsciously preserved scarcity patterns to maintain emotional familiarity and personal identity consistency.

Trevor's transformation began after a routine conversation with a longtime customer who noticed his frustration about repeated financial setbacks. The customer, a retired business owner, shared his own experience with financial cycles that mirrored Trevor's pattern of progress followed by regression. He explained how emotional comfort with crisis prevented him from building sustainable wealth until he confronted his relationship with scarcity. Trevor began reflecting on how his financial decisions often occurred during periods of emotional discomfort rather than genuine necessity. Through financial coaching, he learned to pause major purchases and evaluate whether his motivations were practical or emotional. Trevor gradually developed confidence in maintaining stability, allowing his savings to grow beyond emergency levels without creating subconscious pressure to spend. Marissa experienced her breakthrough when she attended a family gathering where her parents expressed pride in her achievements and encouraged her to pursue opportunities they had never been able to experience. Their support challenged her belief that financial comfort dishonored her upbringing. Marissa began allowing herself to invest in personal goals such as home improvement and travel, discovering that experiencing stability strengthened her emotional well-being and deepened her appreciation for her family's sacrifices.

Scarcity comfort demonstrates how financial trauma can influence behavior long after external circumstances improve. Trevor and Marissa both learned that healing required redefining their relationship with stability and abundance. Trevor discovered that maintaining savings and long-term planning did not eliminate his resilience but expanded his capacity for security and growth. Marissa realized that enjoying financial stability honored her family's sacrifices by transforming survival into progress rather than repeating limitation. Their journeys reveal that scarcity is not simply a financial condition but an emotional environment shaped by early experiences and reinforced by social validation. Occasionally, moments of reflection helped both Trevor and Marissa recognize that releasing attachment to struggle allowed them to experience a deeper sense of peace and purpose, suggesting that abundance often requires individuals to become comfortable with stability rather than crisis.

Understanding why scarcity can feel emotionally familiar reveals one of the subtlest barriers to financial healing. Individuals shaped by financial trauma may unconsciously recreate environments that mirror their past because familiarity provides a sense of control. Healing requires developing comfort with stability and recognizing that abundance does not erase resilience but transforms it into opportunity. As this journey continues, the next chapter will explore the process of reparenting the financial self, examining how individuals can provide emotional safety and guidance to the parts of themselves shaped by early financial trauma, allowing them to build stability with confidence and compassion.

Reparenting Your Financial Self

Marcus had always believed that adulthood meant leaving childhood behind, including the financial chaos that shaped his early years. He built a stable career in property management, paid his bills on time, and prided himself on avoiding debt whenever possible. From an external perspective, Marcus appeared financially responsible, yet his internal reactions to money revealed unresolved fear that quietly influenced his decisions. Whenever unexpected expenses arose, Marcus experienced intense anxiety that felt disproportionate to the situation. He often postponed necessary financial conversations with his partner and avoided long-term financial planning because discussing future commitments triggered memories of instability he had witnessed growing up. Marcus was raised in a household where financial stress dominated family interactions, and emotional reassurance was often replaced by urgency and tension. As an adult, he unconsciously carried those emotional patterns, responding to financial challenges with the same fear-driven instincts he developed as a child. Marcus believed maturity meant suppressing those reactions rather than understanding them, never realizing that healing required learning how to provide himself with the emotional safety he lacked during his formative years.

Reparenting the financial self involves recognizing that many financial habits are shaped by childhood experiences rather than conscious adult decisions. When individuals grow up in financially unstable environments, they often develop emotional coping mechanisms designed to protect them from fear and uncertainty. These coping strategies can include avoidance, over control, emotional spending, or chronic anxiety around financial planning. Reparenting means intentionally replacing fear-based responses with guidance, reassurance, and stability that mirror the supportive structure individuals needed but may not have received. Marcus began understanding this concept after attending a couple's financial workshop where the facilitator explained how childhood financial experiences influence adult behavior. He realized that his anxiety during financial discussions was not a reflection of his partner's expectations but a response to unresolved memories of watching his parents argue about overdue bills. Reparenting requires individuals to recognize that the fearful voice guiding their financial reactions often belongs to a younger version of themselves seeking safety rather than sabotage. By acknowledging that internal dialogue, individuals can begin replacing criticism with encouragement and fear with confidence.

Sophia experienced the need for financial reparenting through a different emotional journey. Growing up in a household where financial independence was celebrated but emotional support was limited, Sophia learned to rely entirely on herself when facing challenges. She developed exceptional self-sufficiency, building a successful career as a freelance software developer and managing her finances without external assistance. However, Sophia struggled with chronic burnout caused by her refusal to seek support or delegate responsibilities. She associated asking for help with weakness, a belief reinforced during childhood when family members praised her independence but rarely offered emotional reassurance. Sophia's financial habits reflected this pattern, as she avoided hiring professional advisors or discussing financial strategies with trusted mentors. She maintained complete control over her finances but carried the emotional burden alone, leading to decision fatigue and stress. Reparenting her financial self, required Sophia to redefine independence as the ability to make empowered choices rather than isolation from support systems. She learned that providing herself with emotional reassurance included allowing guidance and collaboration without perceiving them as threats to her autonomy.

Reparenting financial behavior involves developing internal leadership that replaces fear-driven instincts with intentional decision-making. Marcus began practicing this transformation by approaching financial planning conversations with curiosity rather than avoidance. He worked with a financial advisor who encouraged him to view budgeting as a tool for empowerment rather than restriction. Marcus gradually reframed his perspective, recognizing that planning for the future created stability rather than reminding him of past instability. He also began practicing emotional regulation techniques, allowing himself to pause and reflect when financial anxiety surfaced rather than reacting impulsively. Sophia's reparenting process involved building trust in collaborative financial planning. She began working with a tax consultant and investment advisor, learning that strategic partnerships strengthened her financial security while reducing emotional stress. Both Marcus and Sophia discovered that reparenting requires patience and consistency because emotional patterns formed during childhood cannot be replaced through information alone. Transformation occurs when individuals repeatedly demonstrate to themselves that financial decisions can be made from confidence rather than fear, gradually building emotional safety through intentional action.

Empowerment becomes the central outcome of financial reparenting because individuals learn to replace survival instincts with leadership and vision. Marcus began setting financial goals aligned with his long-term aspirations rather than focusing solely on avoiding financial crisis. He and his partner developed shared financial plans that strengthened their relationship and reduced emotional tension during money discussions. Marcus discovered that providing himself with emotional reassurance allowed him to approach financial decisions with clarity and optimism. Sophia experienced empowerment by redefining success as sustainable balance rather than relentless productivity. By building financial systems that included professional guidance and personal boundaries, she created stability that supported both her career growth and emotional well-being. Their journeys illustrate that reparenting is not about erasing past experiences but about transforming how individuals respond to them. Occasionally, moments of reflection helped Marcus and Sophia recognize that treating themselves with patience and encouragement allowed them to develop confidence they had previously sought through external validation, suggesting that emotional leadership often becomes the foundation for sustainable financial growth.

Reparenting the financial self represents a shift from reacting to past trauma toward actively shaping future stability. Individuals who embrace this process learn to approach financial challenges with resilience and intentional strategy rather than fear or avoidance. Marcus and Sophia both discovered that healing financial trauma required acknowledging their younger emotional experiences while empowering their adult decision-making abilities. Their transformation demonstrates that financial stability is not created solely through income or discipline but through emotional confidence that allows individuals to trust themselves as capable stewards of their resources. Occasionally, subtle moments of gratitude helped them recognize that their progress reflected not only personal growth but also the culmination of resilience developed during challenging life seasons.

Understanding reparenting prepares individuals to embrace identity transformation fully, allowing them to rewrite financial narratives shaped by fear and replace them with confidence, clarity, and purpose.

As this journey continues, the next chapter will explore rewriting financial identity, examining how individuals transition from survival-based self-perception toward empowered self-belief and how identity transformation becomes the foundation for sustainable wealth and personal fulfillment.

Rewriting Your Financial Identity

Naomi stood in her newly expanded studio late one evening, reviewing client designs while watching her team prepare materials for upcoming events. Just two years earlier, she had resisted the idea of hiring employees, convinced that expanding her business would expose her to risks she was not prepared to manage. Now, she found herself leading a growing creative company that allowed her to work fewer hours while generating significantly more income. Despite her progress, Naomi occasionally felt moments of disbelief, questioning whether her success was sustainable or simply temporary fortune. Those thoughts reminded her of earlier years when she declined opportunities because she feared transformation would require abandoning the cautious identity that protected her during financial uncertainty. Naomi realized that her greatest challenge had never been learning business strategies but learning to see herself as someone capable of maintaining success. Her external growth required an internal shift, forcing her to confront long-standing beliefs about worth, stability, and personal capability. Naomi's journey illustrates how financial healing ultimately requires rewriting identity narratives that shape decision-making and emotional responses to opportunity.

Financial identity represents the internal story individuals tell themselves about their relationship with money, success, and personal value. These narratives are often formed during childhood through observation, emotional experiences, and cultural messaging. Naomi grew up believing stability was fragile and success required constant vigilance, beliefs that initially protected her from disappointment but later limited her professional expansion. Many individuals shaped by financial trauma carry similar identity scripts, viewing themselves as survivors rather than builders or believing wealth is reserved for people with different backgrounds or privileges. These internal narratives influence career choices, spending behaviors, and investment decisions, often creating invisible limitations that persist even when external circumstances improve. Rewriting financial identity requires individuals to recognize that past experiences shaped their coping strategies but do not determine their future potential. Naomi began this transformation by intentionally challenging self-doubt whenever it surfaced, replacing fear-based assumptions with evidence of her growth and capability. Over time, she developed confidence rooted not in external validation but in internal recognition of her resilience and adaptability.

Elena, whose emotional spending once provided temporary relief from workplace stress and personal loneliness, experienced her own identity transformation through consistent emotional and financial awareness. After implementing structured financial planning and developing healthier coping strategies, Elena gradually built savings and reduced impulsive spending habits. Yet her greatest transformation occurred when she began viewing herself as someone capable of long-term stability rather than someone vulnerable to emotional financial decisions. Elena noticed that her internal dialogue shifted from questioning whether she could maintain financial discipline to assuming she was capable of intentional stewardship. This shift influenced her professional confidence, allowing her to pursue leadership opportunities she previously avoided due to fear of additional responsibility. Financial identity transformation often extends beyond money management, influencing how individuals perceive their competence, authority, and ability to navigate complex life decisions. Elena's progress demonstrated that rewriting financial identity creates ripple effects that strengthen multiple areas of personal and professional development.

Rewriting identity requires intentional repetition of empowering beliefs supported by consistent behavior. Naomi reinforced her new identity by implementing business systems that allowed her to delegate responsibilities confidently while maintaining creative control. Each successful project managed by her team strengthened her belief that leadership expanded her influence rather than threatened her independence. Elena reinforced her identity by maintaining financial routines that aligned with her long-term goals, demonstrating to herself that discipline could coexist with emotional well-being. These repeated actions created evidence that contradicted their earlier survival-based narratives, gradually replacing fear-driven self-perception with empowerment-based identity. Financial trauma often creates deeply ingrained beliefs that can only be replaced through consistent demonstration of new patterns. Naomi and Elena both discovered that confidence grows through action rather than waiting for fear to disappear. Occasionally, moments of reflection helped them recognize that their progress reflected not luck but intentional transformation, suggesting that identity rewriting involves acknowledging growth while trusting continued development.

Calvin also experienced identity transformation as he learned to redefine success beyond constant achievement. After embracing balanced career growth and prioritizing emotional stability, Calvin noticed that his professional performance improved while his anxiety decreased. He began mentoring younger colleagues, recognizing similarities between their fears and his earlier struggles with self-worth and financial validation. Mentorship reinforced Calvin's identity as someone capable of guiding others rather than competing for approval, further strengthening his confidence and sense of purpose. Financial identity rewriting often involves embracing roles that reflect growth, such as leadership, mentorship, or community influence. These roles provide opportunities to practice new self-perceptions while contributing to broader impact. Calvin discovered that success became more fulfilling when it aligned with purpose rather than proving worth, illustrating how identity transformation enhances both personal satisfaction and professional effectiveness.

Rewriting financial identity is not about denying past experiences but integrating them into a narrative that emphasizes growth rather than limitation. Naomi acknowledged that her caution developed from genuine financial vulnerability but recognized that her present environment allowed for expansion. Elena accepted that emotional spending once provided necessary comfort but embraced new strategies that supported stability and self-respect. Calvin recognized that his drive for achievement originated from survival instincts but transformed that drive into purposeful leadership. Their journeys reveal that identity transformation requires compassion for past experiences combined with courage to embrace new possibilities. Occasionally, subtle moments of gratitude helped them recognize that their evolving identities reflected both personal determination and the resilience developed through earlier challenges, reinforcing the understanding that transformation often emerges from the willingness to reinterpret past adversity as preparation for future opportunity.

Understanding financial identity transformation marks a critical stage in healing because it shifts the foundation of decision-making from fear to confidence. Individuals who rewrite their internal narratives begin pursuing opportunities aligned with long-term stability and personal fulfillment rather than short-term emotional reassurance. Naomi, Elena, and Calvin demonstrate that financial healing is sustained when individuals believe they are capable of maintaining success and deserving of stability. As this journey continues, the next chapter will explore building safety as a foundation for wealth, examining how emotional and financial security create the stability necessary for sustainable prosperity and how developing internal safety allows individuals to embrace abundance without fear of losing it.

Building Safety Before Building Wealth

Elena stood at the window of her apartment one quiet Sunday morning, watching sunlight stretch across the city skyline while reviewing her financial dashboard on her tablet. The screen displayed numbers she once believed were impossible to achieve, including a growing emergency fund, retirement contributions, and a modest investment portfolio. Despite the evidence of stability, Elena noticed something surprising. For the first time in her adult life, she did not feel anxious while reviewing her finances. The absence of fear felt unfamiliar, almost unsettling, as if her mind expected tension that never arrived. Elena remembered earlier years when checking her bank balance felt like bracing for impact, preparing emotionally for disappointment or financial crisis. Her transformation did not occur through income increase alone but through consistent efforts to create emotional safety around money. Elena learned that financial healing required teaching her mind and body to trust stability, allowing her to approach wealth building without subconscious fear undermining her progress. Her journey demonstrated that safety must exist before wealth can be sustained because individuals cannot hold abundance when their internal environment remains conditioned for survival.

Financial safety extends beyond emergency savings or stable income; it involves creating emotional confidence that allows individuals to interact with money without fear-driven decision-making. Many individuals attempt to build wealth while their subconscious remains anchored in financial trauma, leading to behaviors that sabotage progress despite strong financial knowledge. Elena initially struggled with this conflict when she began saving consistently, noticing that her anxiety increased whenever her savings reached milestones she once considered secure. She realized that stability felt unfamiliar because her childhood experiences conditioned her to expect financial disruption. Building safety required consistent reinforcement that stability could be maintained through intentional planning rather than constant vigilance. Elena practiced financial routines that created predictability, such as scheduled financial reviews and automatic transfers to savings accounts, gradually teaching her nervous system that stability could be sustained. Financial safety emerges when individuals replace reactive financial habits with consistent, intentional behaviors that reinforce trust in their ability to manage resources effectively. Trevor, whose financial cycles previously reflected subconscious comfort with scarcity, also began learning the importance of safety as a foundation for growth. After recognizing his pattern of undermining savings through impulsive spending, Trevor worked with a financial coach to develop structured financial goals aligned with long-term stability rather than short-term gratification. Trevor discovered that building safety involved creating financial systems that reduced emotional pressure, including separate accounts for discretionary spending and long-term investments. Initially, Trevor felt discomfort maintaining savings without spending them because his identity was shaped by solving financial emergencies rather than preventing them. Over time, consistent success in maintaining financial stability allowed Trevor to experience confidence that replaced his subconscious attachment to crisis. He began pursuing professional certifications that increased his earning potential, recognizing that safety provided the emotional stability necessary to pursue growth opportunities he once avoided. Trevor's transformation illustrates how emotional safety expands financial capacity by allowing individuals to focus on strategic development rather than reactive problem-solving.

Building financial safety also requires establishing relational and psychological support systems that reinforce stability. Calvin experienced this transformation as he balanced professional advancement with emotional well-being, recognizing that financial success alone did not guarantee security. After redefining his relationship with achievement, Calvin began prioritizing relationships and mentorship that supported both his career and personal growth. He created financial plans that included charitable giving and family investment strategies, aligning his wealth-building efforts with purpose and community impact. These decisions strengthened Calvin's emotional connection to his financial goals, reinforcing stability through meaningful direction rather than performance-driven anxiety. Financial safety often emerges when individuals align wealth with values and purpose, allowing money to function as a tool for fulfillment rather than validation. Calvin discovered that sharing financial knowledge through mentorship reinforced his confidence and strengthened his sense of identity as someone capable of sustaining success while contributing to others' growth.

Sophia also embraced financial safety by redefining independence as the ability to create sustainable balance rather than complete self-reliance. After developing collaborative financial planning systems, Sophia noticed a significant reduction in stress and decision fatigue, allowing her to focus on expanding her software development career strategically. She implemented structured income management practices that accounted for freelance income variability, creating financial predictability that replaced her previous cycles of overwork and burnout. Sophia's transformation demonstrated that financial safety includes trusting support systems and professional guidance, recognizing that stability often requires collaboration rather than isolation. Occasionally, moments of reflection helped Sophia recognize that emotional reassurance she once sought through excessive independence was now replaced by confidence in her ability to manage both resources and relationships effectively. Her journey illustrates how financial safety strengthens resilience by allowing individuals to navigate challenges with confidence rather than fear.

Building safety before wealth requires individuals to recognize that financial trauma often conditions them to focus on survival rather than sustainability. Elena, Trevor, Calvin, and Sophia each discovered that stability emerges when emotional confidence supports financial planning, allowing individuals to interact with money without subconscious resistance. Financial safety allows individuals to pursue investment opportunities, career advancement, and personal fulfillment with clarity and intentionality. Occasionally, subtle spiritual reflection helped them recognize that peace often emerges when individuals trust their ability to steward resources responsibly, reinforcing the understanding that financial healing involves both emotional growth and purposeful vision. Their journeys demonstrate that safety is not a passive condition but an active commitment to creating environments that support long-term stability and personal empowerment.

Understanding financial safety prepares individuals to embrace abundance without fear of losing it, creating a foundation for visionary growth and legacy building. When individuals feel secure internally and externally, they gain the confidence necessary to pursue opportunities aligned with their purpose and values. As this journey continues, the next chapter will explore learning to receive without guilt, examining how individuals shaped by financial trauma often struggle to accept prosperity and how embracing abundance becomes an essential step toward building generational stability and fulfilling their highest potential.

Learning to Receive Without Guilt

Marissa sat quietly in her newly purchased home, running her fingers across the polished wooden table she once believed she would never own. The house represented years of disciplined saving, career growth, and careful financial planning, yet she found herself struggling to feel the joy she expected when she finally achieved homeownership. Instead of celebration, Marissa experienced subtle waves of guilt that surfaced whenever she admired the comfort and beauty surrounding her. She remembered childhood evenings when her parents postponed personal desires to ensure bills were paid, often reminding her that survival required sacrifice. Those lessons shaped her understanding of responsibility and resilience, but they also created a subconscious belief that comfort must be earned through prolonged struggle. As Marissa walked through her home, she noticed how frequently she questioned whether she deserved such stability, as if abundance required justification. Her experience revealed one of the most overlooked consequences of financial trauma: individuals who spend years learning how to survive often struggle to receive prosperity when it arrives. Receiving abundance requires emotional permission that many individuals were never taught to grant themselves. Financial trauma frequently conditions individuals to associate prosperity with guilt or fear because abundance represents unfamiliar territory that challenges survival-based identity. Marissa had spent years mastering discipline, budgeting, and delayed gratification, believing those sacrifices would eventually create peace. When stability arrived, she discovered that financial healing required more than strategy; it required embracing abundance without emotional conflict. Many individuals raised in environments defined by scarcity develop subconscious beliefs that enjoying financial comfort dishonors the sacrifices of previous generations. Marissa worried that her success might appear insensitive to her parents' struggles, creating internal tension that diminished her ability to celebrate her achievements. Learning to receive abundance requires redefining success as continuation of generational progress rather than abandonment of generational sacrifice. Marissa began understanding that her parents' perseverance was intended to create opportunities they never had, and embracing those opportunities honored their resilience rather than erasing it. Receiving prosperity becomes an act of gratitude when individuals recognize that their stability represents the fulfillment of dreams carried by those who came before them.

Trevor also confronted emotional resistance to receiving abundance when his consistent financial planning began producing results that exceeded his expectations. After years of fluctuating savings and reactive spending patterns, Trevor built a substantial emergency fund, secured long-term investments, and achieved professional certifications that increased his earning potential. Despite these accomplishments, Trevor noticed lingering discomfort when considering lifestyle improvements such as upgrading his home or reducing overtime work hours. He feared that relaxing his work intensity would jeopardize the stability he worked tirelessly to achieve. Trevor's internal conflict reflected a belief that abundance must be constantly defended through relentless effort. Financial trauma often creates subconscious associations between security and exhaustion, convincing individuals that prosperity requires continuous struggle to maintain. Trevor began recognizing that receiving abundance meant trusting the systems and discipline he developed rather than relying solely on physical effort. He gradually allowed himself to experience rest and personal fulfillment, discovering that emotional balance strengthened his financial decision-making and professional performance.

Learning to receive without guilt involves embracing the spiritual and emotional truth that prosperity is not punishment for past struggle but restoration from it. Occasionally, moments of quiet reflection helped Marissa recognize that her stability allowed her to support her parents in ways they never expected, including assisting with medical expenses and creating opportunities for family experiences they had long postponed. These acts of generosity transformed her perception of abundance from personal privilege to collective blessing, reinforcing the understanding that receiving prosperity often expands an individual's capacity to uplift others. Trevor experienced similar transformation when he began mentoring younger technicians entering his profession, sharing both technical skills and financial wisdom. He realized that his stability allowed him to guide others away from financial cycles he once struggled to break, demonstrating how receiving abundance can create ripple effects that extend beyond personal achievement. Spiritual reflection occasionally reminded both Marissa and Trevor that growth and restoration often arrive when individuals accept prosperity as part of their journey rather than resisting it through guilt or fear. Calvin also experienced emotional growth in learning to receive success without attaching it to constant performance. After redefining his career priorities, Calvin noticed that he initially struggled to accept recognition and leadership opportunities that acknowledged his professional growth. He feared that visible success would increase expectations he might not sustain, reflecting deep-rooted insecurity shaped by financial trauma. Through mentorship and personal reflection, Calvin began embracing recognition as evidence of growth rather than pressure for perfection. He allowed himself to celebrate achievements and pursue leadership roles aligned with his purpose of guiding others toward financial and professional stability. Calvin discovered that receiving success strengthened his ability to lead authentically because it allowed him to operate from confidence rather than fear. His transformation illustrates how receiving abundance involves accepting personal value and trusting that growth can be sustained through intentional stewardship rather than constant anxiety.

Learning to receive without guilt requires individuals to release survival identities that equate struggle with virtue and abundance with vulnerability. Marissa, Trevor, and Calvin each discovered that prosperity becomes meaningful when it is embraced with gratitude, humility, and purpose. Occasionally, spiritual reflection helped them recognize that receiving abundance often aligns individuals with opportunities to create impact, suggesting that prosperity is not solely a personal reward but a resource for transformation and contribution. Their journeys demonstrate that financial healing involves not only learning how to build wealth but learning how to experience it fully without emotional resistance. Receiving abundance becomes an act of faith in one's growth and resilience, allowing individuals to step into stability with confidence and generosity.

Understanding how to receive prosperity prepares individuals to embrace visionary growth and legacy building, creating a foundation for impact that extends beyond personal achievement. When individuals release guilt and fear surrounding abundance, they gain the emotional freedom necessary to pursue purpose-driven goals and generational transformation. As this journey continues, the next chapter will explore becoming whole, examining how emotional healing, identity transformation, and spiritual alignment create a unified vision that allows individuals to build wealth, purpose, and legacy with clarity and confidence.

The Blueprint to Becoming Whole

Naomi stood alone inside a ballroom moment before one of the largest events her company had ever designed was scheduled to begin. Crystal chandeliers shimmered above tables arranged with intricate décor her team had spent months creating, each detail reflecting the level of excellence she once believed she could never sustain. As she walked slowly across the polished floor, Naomi remembered the version of herself who once declined opportunities out of fear that growth would overwhelm her identity. The transformation surrounding her was not simply the result of business success but the visible evidence of emotional healing that allowed her to step into leadership without fear of losing herself. Naomi realized that wholeness was not perfection or the absence of struggle but the integration of every lesson she had learned through survival, fear, and restoration. She recognized that the strength she developed during seasons of financial instability had prepared her to steward abundance with wisdom rather than anxiety. In that moment, Naomi understood that becoming whole meant accepting every chapter of her journey as preparation for the responsibility of building something larger than personal success.

Wholeness emerges when individuals align emotional healing, identity transformation, and purposeful vision into a unified life direction. Financial trauma often fragments identity, causing individuals to separate survival instincts from personal dreams and spiritual calling. Naomi once believed she needed to choose between safety and expansion, between protecting herself and pursuing opportunity. Through healing, she discovered that wholeness required integrating resilience with ambition, allowing both caution and confidence to coexist. Many individuals shaped by financial trauma struggle with fragmented identities that limit their ability to pursue visionary goals. They may excel professionally while feeling emotionally insecure or achieve financial stability while lacking purpose. The blueprint to becoming whole requires recognizing that financial healing is not solely about money but about aligning personal identity with divine and personal purpose. Naomi's journey demonstrated that wholeness transforms financial success into a platform for impact, allowing individuals to build wealth that reflects both personal fulfillment and generational transformation.

Calvin experienced his own moment of wholeness during a leadership conference where he delivered a keynote presentation on sustainable success and mentorship. Standing before an audience of professionals navigating their own financial and career challenges, Calvin reflected on the years he spent chasing achievement to prove his worth. He recognized that his greatest transformation occurred when he shifted from proving himself to empowering others. Calvin's financial growth allowed him to create scholarship programs and mentorship initiatives designed to support individuals entering professional industries without guidance or financial stability. His journey revealed that wholeness often expands individuals' influence beyond personal achievement, transforming success into a resource for community upliftment. Financial trauma frequently teaches individuals to focus on personal survival, but healing expands perspective, allowing them to recognize their potential to influence others' journeys. Calvin's experience illustrates how becoming whole involves embracing leadership roles that reflect both personal growth and responsibility to create pathways for those who follow.

The blueprint to wholeness requires individuals to redefine wealth as multidimensional, encompassing emotional peace, spiritual alignment, relational strength, and financial stewardship. Trevor discovered this integration as he balanced career advancement with personal fulfillment, recognizing that stability allowed him to pursue passions he once postponed due to survival pressure. Trevor invested in community automotive training programs that provided mentorship and certification opportunities for individuals seeking trade careers. His transformation demonstrated that wholeness often inspires individuals to invest in systems that create generational opportunity rather than focusing solely on personal security. Sophia experienced wholeness through balanced independence and collaboration, building a software development company that prioritized employee well-being alongside financial growth. She recognized that financial stability allowed her to create workplace environments that reflected the emotional support she once lacked, transforming her professional success into a legacy of empowerment. Occasionally, moments of spiritual reflection helped these individuals recognize that wholeness often reveals itself through the realization that personal healing creates opportunities to contribute to collective transformation.

Becoming whole requires embracing a vision that extends beyond immediate financial goals and acknowledges the responsibility that accompanies prosperity. Naomi, Calvin, Trevor, and Sophia each discovered that healing financial trauma allowed them to see their success as part of a larger narrative of restoration and impact. They learned that financial wholeness involves recognizing wealth as a stewardship responsibility that influences families, communities, and future generations. Their journeys reveal that individuals who heal financial trauma often become catalysts for broader transformation, inspiring others to pursue stability and purpose with courage and clarity. Occasionally, subtle spiritual awareness reminded them that their growth aligned with opportunities designed to expand their influence and create legacy beyond personal achievement.

The blueprint to becoming whole requires individuals to accept that their journey from survival to stability positions them as architects of generational change, capable of building structures of opportunity and empowerment that extend far beyond their personal story.

Wholeness represents the culmination of emotional healing, identity transformation, and visionary purpose. It allows individuals to stand confidently in environments they once feared, recognizing that their growth prepared them to steward success with wisdom and humility. Naomi standing in her ballroom, Calvin mentoring future leaders, Trevor building trade mentorship programs, and Sophia designing supportive professional environments demonstrate that becoming whole transforms individuals into builders of legacy and opportunity. Their journeys illustrate that financial healing is not simply about escaping struggle but about stepping into responsibility to create transformation for others. As this journey reaches its final chapter, readers will be invited to embrace the ultimate vision of generational legacy, recognizing that healing financial trauma positions them to rewrite family history, build enduring prosperity, and fulfill a destiny that extends beyond personal achievement into generational restoration and impact.

The Legacy of Healed Wealth

Calvin stood in the front row of a university auditorium, watching as a young woman stepped across the graduation stage to receive her degree in business administration. The moment felt surreal, not because he knew her personally, but because he recognized the significance of what her achievement represented. She was one of several students funded through a scholarship program he created years earlier, inspired by his own journey navigating professional environments without financial or mentorship support. As applause filled the room, Calvin felt a quiet realization settle into his heart. The wealth he once chased to prove his worth had evolved into something far greater than personal success. It had become a bridge connecting his survival story to someone else's opportunity story. Calvin reflected on the nights he spent doubting his ability to sustain success, fearing that one financial misstep could unravel everything he had built. Now he understood that healing financial trauma was never meant to end with personal stability; it was meant to create generational pathways where survival stories transformed into opportunity narratives for those who followed. In that moment, Calvin realized that legacy is not defined by the amount of wealth accumulated but by the number of lives empowered through the stability one chooses to build.

Healed wealth carries a different emotional and spiritual weight than wealth pursued through survival alone. Individuals shaped by financial trauma often pursue stability with urgency, believing security must be captured before it disappears. Healing transforms that urgency into stewardship, allowing individuals to recognize wealth as a resource entrusted to them for purposeful impact. Naomi experienced this realization while overseeing the expansion of her creative company into multiple cities, employing designers, event planners, and coordinators who once struggled to find stable employment opportunities. She often reflected on the early years when she feared growth would overwhelm her identity, never imagining that her business would become a platform creating stability for families beyond her own. Naomi began implementing leadership development programs within her company, teaching financial literacy and entrepreneurship principles to her employees. She recognized that healed wealth extends influence beyond personal lifestyle, creating environments where others gain access to opportunities that once felt unattainable. Healed wealth transforms individuals into architects of stability, building structures that support not only their success but the advancement of communities and future generations.

Trevor witnessed the generational power of healed wealth when he opened his automotive training center designed to provide certification programs for individuals seeking career paths in skilled trades. Standing in the garage during the facility's grand opening, Trevor remembered his early career navigating financial cycles that repeatedly undermined his progress. He understood that his transformation from scarcity comfort to stability confidence allowed him to build something that changed the trajectory for individuals who once felt limited by lack of opportunity. Trevor's training center offered affordable certification programs, mentorship, and job placement partnerships with automotive companies, creating career pathways that provided sustainable income and long-term financial stability for participants. Watching young trainees gain confidence and professional direction reinforced Trevor's understanding that healed wealth multiplies impact through intentional investment in others' growth. Occasionally, he reflected on how financial trauma once taught him to focus on personal survival, realizing that healing expanded his vision to include generational empowerment that extended far beyond his own financial security.

Sophia also embraced the legacy of healed wealth by developing technology programs that provided free coding education and career mentorship for underserved communities. Her company created scholarship opportunities and training initiatives designed to bridge the gap between technical education and employment placement. Sophia often shared her story of overcoming financial avoidance and independence-driven burnout, encouraging students to pursue success while building supportive systems that reinforced sustainability and emotional balance. She recognized that healed wealth allowed her to create environments where individuals could pursue professional dreams without sacrificing emotional well-being. Sophia's initiatives demonstrated that financial healing often reveals purpose-driven missions that align personal success with community transformation. Spiritual reflection occasionally reminded her that prosperity often expands when individuals use their resources to create opportunities that uplift others, reinforcing the understanding that legacy emerges when wealth is guided by purpose rather than accumulation alone.

The legacy of healed wealth extends beyond programs, businesses, or financial investments; it lives within the emotional environments individuals create for their families and future generations. Elena experienced this transformation while teaching her younger niece basic financial planning principles, sharing lessons about emotional spending and intentional stewardship that she once struggled to learn through personal experience. Watching her niece approach money with confidence and curiosity, Elena realized that generational healing begins with conversations that replace fear with empowerment. Financial trauma often teaches families to avoid money discussions or associate them with stress and conflict. Healed wealth transforms those conversations into opportunities for education, encouragement, and emotional security. Elena understood that her transformation from emotional spending to financial confidence created a legacy of emotional and financial literacy that would influence her family for generations. Occasionally, moments of spiritual gratitude helped her recognize that healing personal wounds often opens pathways for generational restoration, reinforcing the belief that legacy is built through both financial stability and emotional empowerment.

Healed wealth carries responsibility because it transforms individuals into guardians of opportunity, entrusted with the ability to rewrite generational narratives shaped by scarcity and survival. Calvin, Naomi, Trevor, Sophia, and Elena each discovered that financial healing positioned them to influence systems, communities, and families in ways they never imagined possible. Their journeys reveal that wealth becomes legacy when it is guided by intentional purpose and visionary stewardship. Healed wealth empowers individuals to invest in education, mentorship, community development, and family stability, creating ripple effects that extend beyond measurable financial success. Occasionally, spiritual awareness reminds individuals that prosperity often aligns with opportunities to create restoration and transformation, reinforcing the belief that financial healing is part of a greater narrative designed to expand opportunity across generations.

Now, reader, the story that has unfolded throughout these pages is no longer only about Marcus, Naomi, Calvin, Elena, Trevor, Sophia, or anyone else whose journey reflected the path from survival to restoration. Their stories were mirrors reflecting the truth of your own potential transformation. Every fear you have carried, every financial mistake you have regretted, every moment you doubted your worth has been part of a story still being rewritten. You are not defined by the seasons where survival felt like your only option. You are defined by the courage you are choosing right now to heal, rebuild, and rise beyond the limitations that once shaped your identity. You are not simply learning how to manage money; you are learning how to transform your relationship with worth, stability, and purpose. The work you are doing is not temporary self-improvement. It is generational reconstruction.

- You are the one your bloodline has been waiting for.

- You are the interruption to cycles of fear, scarcity, and silent struggle.

- You are the architect of stability your ancestors prayed would one day exist.

- You are the steward of opportunities your children will inherit as their foundation rather than their aspiration.

- Your healing is not accidental.

- Your growth is not random.

- Your transformation is not only for you.

- You carry the power to build families where money is discussed with confidence rather than fear.

- You carry the power to create homes where stability is expected rather than hoped for.

- You carry the power to build businesses, careers, and investments that fund opportunity rather than survival.

- You carry the power to create conversations that teach future generations how to manage wealth with wisdom and emotional confidence.

- You carry the power to rewrite narratives that once convinced your family that prosperity belonged to someone else.

- Your story does not end with survival.

- Your story begins with restoration.

- Your journey does not conclude with financial stability.

- Your journey expands into generational transformation.

Stand boldly in the identity you are becoming.

Walk confidently in the stability you are building.

Steward faithfully the opportunities you are receiving.

Build courageously the legacy that will outlive your lifetime.

Because healed wealth is not just money.

Healed wealth is peace.

Healed wealth is freedom.

Healed wealth is generational restoration.

And that legacy begins with **you.**

Other Books by Rev. Darryl Bass

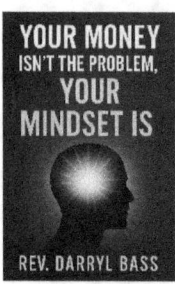

Your Money Isn't the Problem, Your Mindset Is

A transformational work that challenges limiting financial beliefs and redefines wealth from the inside out, empowering readers to align their identity with abundance and responsibility.

This Is Why You're Broke

A bold and unapologetic examination of the habits, beliefs, and financial behaviors that keep people trapped in cycles of struggle. This book confronts uncomfortable truths and replaces excuses with execution, helping readers shift from reactive spending to strategic wealth building.

The Financial Identity Shift

A mindset-and-behavior reset that helps readers align who they are with how they handle money, transforming financial habits through identity-based discipline.

The Life Progression System

A comprehensive blueprint for intentional living, The Life Progression System guides readers through structured personal growth, goal alignment, mindset transformation, and legacy building. It equips individuals with practical tools to move from drifting through life to deliberately designing it.

The Life Progression System Workbook

A companion workbook to the Life Progression System book that allows readers to progress through various tasks, exercises and assignments as they learn.

Financial Progression System

This book provides a step-by-step roadmap to financial stability and long-term wealth building. It teaches readers how to increase income, eliminate debt, build credit, create savings systems, and establish generational financial security.

Borrowed Futures

A wake-up call about the hidden costs of debt and financial shortcuts, showing readers how to escape debt cycles and build futures without financial bondage.

Life Insurance: The Gift of Life After Life

More than a policy explanation, this book reframes life insurance as a strategic wealth-building and legacy-protection tool. It educates families on how to use life insurance for income replacement, debt protection, estate planning, generational wealth transfer, and financial leverage.

The Intellectual Property Wealth Blueprint

A strategic guide to turning knowledge into income, this book teaches creators how to package ideas into books, courses, systems, and assets that generate scalable and recurring revenue streams.

The Intellectual Property Wealth Blueprint 2.0

Focused on licensing, certification, and legacy systems, this volume expands intellectual property into scalable enterprises that create long-term wealth and generational ownership structures.

Coming Soon!

The Overcomer's Wealth Plan

A resilient strategy guide for those rising from adversity, this book outlines disciplined financial recovery, structured planning, and long-term legacy development.

The Blueprint to Becoming Financially Whole

A holistic financial transformation guide that goes beyond budgeting and debt elimination. This book teaches readers how to align mindset, money management, protection strategies, income growth, and legacy planning into one cohesive financial structure built for stability and abundance.

Stewards of Legacy

A leadership and responsibility manifesto focused on generational impact. This book challenges readers to move beyond consumption and become builders—individuals who protect, multiply, and transfer wealth, wisdom, and values to future generations.

The Debt Eliminator

Coming 2026

What if 2026 was the year everything changed?

What if this was the year you stopped surviving... and started building?
The year you stopped juggling bills... and started creating wealth?
The year debt stopped controlling your decisions?

The **Debt Eliminator** is not another budgeting class. It is a structured financial transformation system designed to help individuals and families break free from consumer debt, rebuild financial confidence, and establish a foundation for long-term wealth.

This course was built for hardworking people who are tired of living paycheck to paycheck. It was created for families who want stability, not stress. It was designed for individuals who know they are capable of more—but need a system that works.

What the Debt Eliminator Will Teach You:

• How to eliminate consumer debt strategically and aggressively
• How to increase income without adding overwhelm
• How to rebuild and optimize your credit profile
• How to build savings while eliminating debt
• How to structure emergency funds and protection plans
• How to shift your financial identity from borrower to builder
• How to create systems that prevent debt from returning

This is not theory.
This is execution.

Through step-by-step modules, implementation tools, accountability structure, and real-life application, you will learn how to take control of your money instead of letting it control you.

Imagine waking up without financial anxiety.
Imagine having a plan.
Imagine watching your balances decrease and your confidence increase.
Imagine positioning your household for ownership, investing, and generational legacy.

That transformation begins in 2026.

The Debt Eliminator is more than a course.
It is a movement toward financial clarity, discipline,
and freedom.

Get ready to break cycles.
Get ready to build stability.
Get ready to eliminate debt—permanently.

The Debt Eliminator — Launching 2026.

Join our waiting list Today!
https://savingssolution.org/join

The Financial Freedom Revolution Tour

Launching 2026

This is not a seminar.
This is not a motivational rally.
This is a financial awakening.

The **Financial Freedom Revolution Tour** is a live, high-impact experience designed to ignite transformation in individuals, families, entrepreneurs, and communities ready to break financial cycles and build generational stability.

For too long, people have been working harder but falling further behind. Income rises. Expenses rise. Stress rises. Yet true financial progress feels out of reach.

The Revolution changes that.

This national tour brings together powerful teaching, real strategy, live coaching, and structured execution plans that move attendees from confusion to clarity—and from debt to disciplined wealth-building.

What You'll Experience:

• A clear roadmap to financial stability and long-term wealth
• Step-by-step strategies for eliminating consumer debt
• Income growth frameworks and entrepreneurship positioning
• Credit optimization and financial leverage strategies
• Protection planning and legacy-building principles
• Live financial assessments and actionable implementation steps
• A mindset shift from survival thinking to ownership thinking

This is not inspiration without structure.
This is strategy with accountability.

The Financial Freedom Revolution Tour is built for families who want peace instead of pressure. For entrepreneurs who want profit with structure. For leaders who understand that financial stability is the foundation for community impact.

Imagine thousands gathered in one space—learning, planning, committing to real change.
Imagine leaving with a clear blueprint instead of just excitement.

Imagine knowing exactly what steps to take the next day.

This is more than an event.
It is a declaration that debt cycles end here.
It is a call to financial responsibility, ownership, and generational leadership.

Cities across the country will host this movement in 2026.

Seats will fill.
Lives will shift.
Legacies will be built.

The Financial Freedom Revolution Tour — Coming 2026.

This is the year you stop reacting to money
…and start commanding it.

The revolution begins with one decision.
https://savingssolution.org/tour

Follow on Social Media

Facebook

https://www.facebook.com/LPSCoach

Twitter

https://twitter.com/LPS_Coach

Instagram

https://www.instagram.com/lps_coach/

YouTube

https://www.youtube.com/@life_progressio
n_system

TikTok

https://www.tiktok.com/@debt_annihilator

LinkedIn

https://www.linkedin.com/in/lpscoach/

www.ingramcontent.com/pod-product-compliance
Lightning Source LLC
Chambersburg PA
CBHW071317220526
45468CB00001B/400